HAL•LEONARD
INSTRUMENTAL
PLAY-ALONG

AUDIO
ACCESS
INCLUDED

PLAYBACK+
Speed • Pitch • Balance • Loop

TRUMPET

Disney·PIXAR

Audio arrangements by Peter Deneff

To access audio visit:
www.halleonard.com/mylibrary

Enter Code
7463-7946-8200-8528

ISBN 978-1-5400-2137-3

HAL•LEONARD®
7777 W. BLUEMOUND RD. P.O. BOX 13819 MILWAUKEE, WI 53213

In Australia Contact:
Hal Leonard Australia Pty. Ltd.
4 Lentara Court
Cheltenham, Victoria, 3192 Australia
Email: ausadmin@halleonard.com.au

Visit Hal Leonard Online at
www.halleonard.com

EVERYONE KNOWS JUANITA

from COCO

TRUMPET

Music by GERMAINE FRANCO
Lyrics by ADRIAN MOLINA

MUCH NEEDED ADVICE

from COCO

TRUMPET

Music by MICHAEL GIACCHINO
and GERMAINE FRANCO
Lyrics by ADRIAN MOLINA

LA LLORONA
from COCO

TRUMPET

Traditional Mexican Folksong
Arranged by GERMAINE FRANCO

PROUD CORAZÓN
from COCO

TRUMPET

Music by GERMAINE FRANCO
Lyrics by ADRIAN MOLINA

REMEMBER ME
(Ernesto de la Cruz)
from COCO

Words and Music by KRISTEN ANDERSON-LOPEZ
and ROBERT LOPEZ

TRUMPET

UN POCO LOCO

from COCO

Music by GERMAINE FRANCO
Lyrics by ADRIAN MOLINA

THE WORLD ES MI FAMILIA

from COCO

Music by GERMAINE FRANCO
Lyrics by ADRIAN MOLINA

TRUMPET

Moderately fast, in 2